D0851205

SURVIVAL
FOR
NEW TEACHERS

from

People Who Have Been There

and

Lived to Tell About It

edited by Cheryl Miller Thurston

Cottonwood Press, Inc.

Cottonwood Press, Inc.
109-B Cameron Drive
Fort Collins, Colorado 80525

www.cottonwoodpress.com

ISBN 978-1-877673-85-6

Printed in the United States of America

ACKNOWLEDGMENTS

Cottonwood Press would like to thank the following teachers who have "been there" for their suggestions, tips and advice for new teachers:

Michelle Adams; Youngstown, Florida

Julie Benear; Green, Ohio

Ruth A. Arsenue; Quezon City, Metro Manila, Philippines

Valorie Berryman; Dexter, Michigan

Mary Borg; Greeley, Colorado

Rebecca L. Brown; Williston, North Dakota

Jacci Buelow; Mosinee, Wisconsin

Sandra J. Burdette; Charleston, West Virginia

Margaret Carlock; Lecanto, Florida

Sunshine Copeland; Orange, Texas

Pamela S. Cottrill; Morgantown, West Virginia

Linda L. Crockett; Mansfield, Ohio

Matt Danielson; Montevideo, Minnesota

Esther Davison; Pine Bluffs, Wyoming

Linda DeVille; Rescue, California

Karyl DiPrince; Pueblo, Colorado

Charles A. Eberhard; Pine Bluffs, Wyoming

Charlotte Eichelberger; Hagerstown, Maryland

Janice Ellens; Kalamazoo, Michigan

Joan Endicott; Perry, Oklahoma

Amy Enzi; Gillette, Wyoming

Scott C. Ferguson; Virginia Beach, Virginia

Laurell Fogg; Carpenter, Wyoming

Kristen Frohnhoefer; Ellicott City, Maryland

Vicki Gage; Shepherdsville, Kentucky

Janice M. Gifford; Mt. Olivet, Kentucky

Catherine Gilbert; Baltimore, Maryland

Judith A. Granese; Las Vegas, Nevada

Susie Greenwald; Highland Park, Illinois

Debbie Hartwig; Woodside, California

Mary Harutun; Carbondale, Colorado

Gail Skroback Hennessey; Harpursville, New York

Sara Hess; Tuscola, Illinois

Carolyn Huisjen; Fort Collins, Colorado

Vicki Hurt; Abilene, Texas

Susan Inghram; Chandler, Arizona

Kevin T. Irvine; Fort Collins, Colorado

Pat Jacobson; Cody, Wyoming

Lynn Keber; Loveland, Colorado

Carole Koester; West Palm Beach, California

Katherine Kosareff; Post Falls, Idaho

Randy Larson; Gillette, Wyoming

Ann Lawler-Perry; Fort Collins, Colorado

Lynn Lucke Lutkin; Fort Collins, Colorado

Marty McDougal; Austin, Texas

Joanna M. Martin; St. Charles, Illinois

Polly Miller; La Junta, Colorado

Jeanne Montembeau; Biddeford, Michigan

Paula Muri; Altoona, Pennsylvania

Susan Muse; Charlottesville, Virginia

Shelby Myers-Verhage; Cedar Rapids, Iowa

R.J. Penhallegon; Baltimore, Maryland

Jan Reeder; St. Joseph, Missouri

Siri Regan; New Orleans, Louisiana

Saundra Hayn Schaulis; Sunnyvale, California

Heather Smith; Bartlesville, Oklahoma

Rebecca Snow; Newark, California

Ann Spence; Waterford, Pennsylvania

Arla Squires; Fort Collins, Colorado

Jeff Squires; Fort Collins, Colorado

Suzanne Tingley; Watertown, New York

Dena Tompsett-Hartmann; Fort Collins, Colorado

Amanda Unkle; Dennisville, New Jersey

Shannon Vick; Antioch, California

Leslie Walker; Raton, New Mexico

Marjorie Waterbrook; Tucson, Arizona

Connie Williams; Carlisle, Ohio

Melissa Williams; Andover, Minnesota

Rita Wills; Las Vegas, Nevada

Sharon Wynn; Managua, Nicaragua, Central America

TABLE OF CONTENTS

TO NEW TEACHERS...

I began my first teaching job as a mini-skirted 22-year-old who got into trouble the first day for not having a hall pass. I credit my survival the first couple of years to two young female teachers I admired. "What do you do when a kid says he won't do something?" I would ask Linda. She would give me not only suggestions for what to do but also for the words to use as I did it. Somehow having the words ready ahead of time helped me more than anything. Her advice—and her words—always worked for me.

"Don't walk toward an angry, violent kid," another teacher, Mary, told me one day. "Calmly say what you expect him to do, as if you mean it, and walk away, as if it has never even occurred to you that he wouldn't do what you say. You give him a chance to save face." She was right. I mentally thanked her again and again over the years for that piece of intelligent advice.

Succeeding as a teacher involves a combination of courage, luck, skill, knowledge, sensitivity and persistence. If you are a new teacher, listen to teachers with years of experience. They have learned a few things over the years. Not everything will work for you, but it's smart to pay attention and be open to their advice and help.

We all make mistakes on the job and learn from them, but the mistakes of a new teacher are often particularly difficult. They involve a big audience (the students) and consequences that are difficult or even impossible to correct.

For example, a teacher who makes the mistake of not being consistent enough in classroom management makes that mistake in front of 30 or so young people who are quite aware that he has blown it. That's hard to correct, except by starting over, and it's hard to start over in the middle of the year.

On the other hand, a new teacher's inexperience can often be one of her greatest assets. She looks at everything with new eyes. Because she doesn't know that something "just won't work with these kids," she may go ahead and do it, with great success. She often has an excitement about her new job that is infectious, and she may bring life to a classroom as she experiments and feels her way.

Welcome to the world of teaching. Take a look at the advice in this book, collected from experienced teachers all over the country. I hope that some of these words of wisdom will make your new teaching career just a little bit easier and more successful.

Happy teaching!

Cheryl Miller Thurston

PLANNING AND ORGANIZING

PLANNING
AND
ORGANIZING

Teachers are some of the most organized people in the world. They have to be. If they don't develop a system of planning and organizing that works for them, they flounder, struggle and ultimately sink under the heavy demands.

As a new teacher, you may find that it helps to understand why it seems impossible to keep up with everything. Take a look at the facts:

- A typical secondary teacher supervises 150–180 people per day. (Think of a person in the business world who has that much responsibility. He or she would probably be a top-level manager.) Elementary teachers may supervise fewer individuals, but they are responsible for a wider range of subjects.

- Although a teacher manages huge numbers of people, he or she does it without the benefit of a secretary to do any of the paperwork. A typical manager would have at least one secretary to answer phones, type, photocopy, file, staple, etc. Teachers do not.

- In the business world, people can use time at work to prepare for presentations and meetings. Teachers have very little time to actually plan lessons while at school, and most of them have five or more presentations *every single day.*

- The paperwork is overwhelming. A middle school teacher, with six classes a day of 30 students each, has 180 students. If each of them turns in only three papers or tests per week, that's 540 papers per week to grade and record—a whopping 19,440 papers per year! No wonder they have difficulty keeping up.

Learning to plan and organize efficiently is an important job for new teachers. Don't be afraid to experiment. Listen to advice and pointers from veteran teachers, but adapt their methods to fit *your* style. No two teachers work in exactly the same way. Experiment to see what works best for you.

The tips that follow may help you in learning to plan and organize efficiently.

Expect things to take MORE time than you think they will. A simple little assignment that you think will take 15 minutes may end up taking the whole class period.

Expect things to take a lot LESS time than you think they will. You will sometimes find that what you had planned for two days will take 15 minutes. Then you will be facing 30 students with nothing to do—not a good situation. Always plan more than you think you could possibly need.

You don't have to do things the way the teacher next door does them. If keeping materials in piles works better for you than using file folders, stick to piles.

> # Handle paper only once,
> whenever possible. Fill out forms from the office as you receive them. Decide immediately what to keep and what to throw out.

Take a personal time management course. Unless you are already a genius at time management, it should help.

> **Be prepared to use a lot of time outside school for preparation and grading and worrying. You will probably be shocked and horrified by how much time you will need at first. That's normal.**

Record daily assignments on a clipboard, chart, or website for students to check after they have been absent. **You might also assign each student a "buddy"**—a fellow classmate to check with about assignments.

Have a short **"DO NOW"** activity, puzzle, riddle, or challenging question on the board or overhead for students to complete as soon as they come into class. This allows time for you to take roll, collect homework, talk to a student about missing work, pass out papers, etc. **When students are engaged, they don't have time to act up.**

If you tell a student to correct or redo something, make a note of it. If you forget about it, students will quickly learn they can get away with not doing their assignments. **Keep a daily "owed" list** with the names of students and what they need to do.

Don't be afraid, once in a great while, to "forget" to grade a stack of assignments. If you are totally buried in paper work, it may help you catch up. The world will not end as a result. In fact, the students probably won't even notice.

Put homework and extra copies of handouts in special boxes. Students who have been absent can go to the boxes and pick up what they need when they return to class.

Buy a good quality, roomy **briefcase**—one you love. You will be carrying it back and forth from home a lot.

> **Don't try to "wing it" unless you are extremely good at it. Students know when a teacher is not prepared. Respect your students by using their time well.**

Don't be upset if you have to trash one day's lesson plan because of an unexpected schedule change. That change will seem irrelevant by the time May rolls around.

Keep good notes. Administrators, guidance counselors, parents, etc., constantly turn to teachers for support, help and information about students. An index card on each student, kept in a simple file in a private place, works well. So does a computer file. Be specific, noting dates, incidents, people involved, etc. It's also a good idea to keep a copy of notes you write to parents, students, other teachers and administrators.

Don't think that you are losing your mind if it feels like you can never catch up. You probably can't.

BUILDING RAPPORT
WITH STUDENTS

BUILDING RAPPORT
WITH STUDENTS

"Rapport" is an important word in the world of teaching. Teachers who have good rapport are usually more successful than teachers who don't.

But what is good rapport? It is more than just getting along well with students. It is also respect, a mutual respect between teachers and students.

How do teachers build rapport with students? The tips that follow give some practical advice.

Learn your students' names as quickly as you can—certainly by the end of the first week and sooner if you have only one class. It's easier to say, "Jason, put away your cell phone," than "Hey, you with the curly hair and the nose ring—put away your cell phone." Learning their names promptly will let students know right away that you care about them and that you are serious about your job.

Remember that students don't **care what you know** until they **know that you care**.

Let students see you at **after-school and evening activities**, even if you don't have an assigned duty. It shows that you care about them and your school.

Remember what **YOU** were like when you were the same age as your students.

If you're not from the area where you teach, ask someone who is to give you a tour. Learning about the neighborhoods where they live will help you understand your students better.

Children are not miniature adults. Love them for what they *are*, not for what you want them to be.

Enjoy your students! If you enjoy them, they can tell, and they will enjoy you, too.

**Never forget that students
are the reason you are a teacher.
Do not allow yourself, ever, to start
seeing them as the enemy.**

View hall duty as an opportunity rather than a duty. It gives you a chance to build positive relationships with students outside the classroom. The efforts **out** of the classroom will enhance your rapport **in** the classroom.

Meet students at the door of your classroom. Smile and greet them by name. You will set a welcoming tone. The personal contact will also help build rapport.

Listen to students.

Understand that getting close to students gives them an important reason to succeed—to keep your personal opinion of them positive. Yes, it is better if they do well just to please themselves. However, at least in the beginning, **your opinion** may be all that some students have to lean on.

> **Don't get too hung up
> on the way
> students dress.
> A student can
> have green hair
> and still learn algebra.**

Remember that a student's hope is that he or she stands out, if not in the world, then at least in your eyes. Even when they're older and toughened and wise beyond their years, students still want to be noticed. **They still want to feel important. Notice them.**

Try to talk individually with as many students as you can each day. **A few personal words** will go a long way toward helping you earn respect and good will.

Don't take yourself too seriously.

Pay attention to what movies, TV shows and music your students like. If you know something about their world, you know something about them.

Go the extra mile to connect with students. For example, some teachers send students postcards before school starts, welcoming them to class. They take extra time to write positive comments on papers. They acknowledge birthdays with a greeting card or note. Even the smallest efforts can pay big dividends in reaching students.

Be kind.

Pay attention. Notice and comment on a student's new haircut, funny T-shirt, kind remark. Notice also if a student seems upset or distracted. See if you can help.

Never abuse a student's trust in adults. You are an adult. That means no drinking with students, no flirting with students, no sex with students. Ever. Under any circumstances. Period.

In Your Classroom

IN YOUR CLASSROOM

A teacher's world is the classroom. So much takes place there—joy, disappointment, problems, growth, opportunity, advancement, laughter, tears, frustration, delight and so much more. No teacher experiences the same thing every day. There are highs and lows in teaching, just as there are highs and lows in life.

The tips that follow offer sound advice about the classroom for teachers of all ages and any subject matter.

Display student work. Students love to see their work highlighted; it validates their effort. Include a variety of assignments so that all students have an opportunity to be recognized. Change the displays often.

Smile and laugh with your students. Enjoy them.

Use fabric to cover your bulletin boards. You can find a wide variety of colors and patterns, and it can be used over and over again. Take a picture of your board before you take it down, and store the lettering in a ziplock bag. That way you can use it again next year.

Recognize your power as a teacher.
Use it for good.

Tell your students, "Nobody wants you to succeed as much as I do." Make sure you believe it, and they will, too.

Students learn more through praise than through criticism. Look for the good they do, and applaud them.

> **Undeserved praise is a lie, and students know it. In trying to enhance self-esteem, don't get into the habit of praising what isn't really praiseworthy.**

Rearrange the desks now and then. At the very least, change the seating arrangement from time to time. Sometimes a different seat in the room has an amazing effect on a student's attitude and/or behavior.

Keep reminding yourself, always:
"I am the adult here."

When passing out materials, stand in front of a row and count out the amount you need. Have students pass back the papers. Don't walk around and pass them out individually; it takes too much time and gives students an opportunity to misbehave. (This advice seems simple but it's surprising how many new teachers don't heed it.)

Become as computer savvy as possible. Students respect technical expertise. (Also, the more you know, the less they can get away with!)

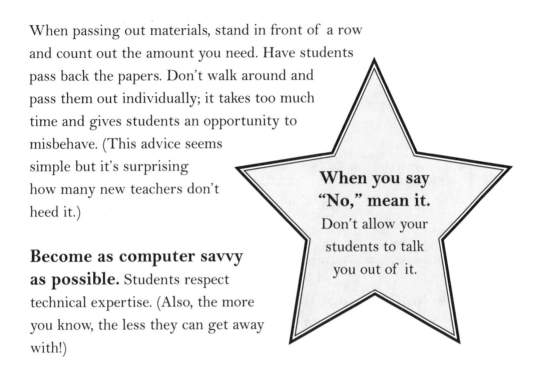

When you say "No," mean it. Don't allow your students to talk you out of it.

Students know busywork when they see it. Don't assign it. Make sure everything you assign has a purpose, and make sure students know the purpose. **(Note: they don't have to agree that the purpose is a good one. They just need to know what it is.)**

Remember that new teachers have no reputation yet. Establish yours carefully. It's easier to develop a good reputation than to repair a bad one. (And if you have a good reputation, next year will be *much* easier than this one!)

Post plenty of instructional sayings around the room, and change them often. Some students are strictly visual learners. If nothing else sinks in all year, a good quotation might.

Set **HIGH** expectations. Your students will rise to your challenges.

Be honest and specific in giving positive feedback to students. Say, "Your second paragraph is really effective in creating a picture," not, "I really love your work." Say, "Your project is very creative and organized," not just, "Good job."

Assume nothing.

Don't try to ingratiate yourself by doing stand-up comedy in class. **Be yourself.**

If you have a hard time justifying a policy, procedure, action or assignment, even to yourself, take a harder look at it. Maybe it needs to be changed.

Monitor computer classwork carefully. Walk around constantly, check the history on each computer, and pay close attention. Know that students are very adept at going to a website you have not approved while keeping another page open to work on an assignment.

Remember that your job is teaching young people. They should be your main focus. **Practice becoming better today than you were yesterday.**

Tell the truth.

During quizzes, **stay nearby**. You can keep the frightened students from making the mistake of cheating. You can tap a dozing student on the shoulder with a pencil or pat a nervous student on the back. You are right there to say, "Good job!" or, "You've only got three more lines."

Don't be surprised that you have to repeat instructions three or four times, or even nine or ten times. Also don't be surprised if, as a result, you sometimes feel like screaming or tearing your hair out. You're perfectly normal.

Smile.

Smile a lot.

Children crave consistency and structure. Provide a safe, structured environment in your classroom. For so many children, the world outside of school is scary and inconsistent, with few boundaries. Establish a routine that they can count on, anticipate, even look forward to.

Make sure your class sees *you* learning, too.

Invest in a camera. Take a lot of photographs of students, and post them.

> **Face the fact that there will be times when nothing works.**
> Teachers deal with quirky human beings, not machine parts.

Post your homework online, and put your school e-mail address on the homework website. If you keep the website up to date, students and parents may be able to answer many questions for themselves, without having to contact you.

Admit when you are wrong. You aren't perfect.

Tell students who you are. Don't give 40-minute talks about your dramatic and glowing past. But if the conversation happens to turn to pets, it's okay to tell them about your beloved but ugly dog Eggo. If the class is talking about horrible Christmas presents, go ahead and tell them about your spouse's habit of giving dismal stocking stuffers, like shoelaces and socks.

Don't plan a test for fire drill day.

> **Textbooks aren't always right—**
>
> **or even interesting.**
>
> **Don't treat them as gospel.**

The last five minutes of class is a good time to let students unwind and gab a little. It is also a good time to listen. **You can learn a lot if you open your ears to what students have to say.**

Don't forget all the students in the middle. The high achievers get attention. The behavior problems get attention. The good students doing ordinary work are often ignored.

Spend more time on things you love. If you love teaching poetry, you may be able to cut another unit a bit short and spend more time on poetry. Students will learn more about the subjects you love.

When it comes to technology, there is sometimes no better resource than your own students.

Focus on the positive. Comment daily in each class about what you like. ("Thank you for waiting quietly." "Wow! You caught on to that right away!" "Nice job of improving your test scores this week.") A little praise goes a long way.

Never, ever forget your **sense of humor.** If a student does something funny, laugh. If a situation is ridiculous, smile at its absurdity. Save up funny stories to tell your family and friends.

Use a color other than red to grade papers. Then it won't look like you bled all over the assignments. (But if you can't find anything except a red pen one night, go ahead and use it. You won't damage anyone's self-esteem forever by using red now and then.)

Remember that school is the best place a lot of kids will ever get to go.

> **Remember that
> every student is worth your effort.
> Some need affection and kindness most
> when they seem to deserve it least.**

Keep things in perspective. If a student writes profanity in a book, it's something to deal with. It's not time to reserve a cell in the penitentiary for the child. Similarly, if your lesson flops, don't berate yourself and look into becoming an accountant instead of a teacher. Learn from your mistakes. Laugh at yourself. Go on.

To feel safe, students need to know that you have things under control. Act like it. If you don't know something and must tell them you will check into it and find out, say it *confidently*. Sometimes you just have to fake it. **Sometimes you have to act like you know what you are doing, even when you don't.**

Present material in many different ways, so that individual learning styles are addressed. A student who can't grasp anything if you **tell** him about it may understand just fine if he gets to **read** an explanation. Some students learn best if there is some sort of physical action involved in the lesson. Others excel when there is a lot of interaction with other people. Some work best by themselves in a peaceful, quiet environment. Vary your lessons and activities as much as possible. Then you are more likely to reach everyone.

Would you want to sit still all day? Don't make your students. Vary your lessons so that students do more than just sit and listen.

**If you are bored,
your students are probably bored.**
Change something. Experiment with
something different. Keep yourself
interested, and the students are likely to
stay interested, too.

Be flexible. Don't fall apart when your lesson doesn't go exactly as planned.

Give students **time to think** after you have asked a question. Wait **a lot longer** than you think you should before you call on anyone. You will give more students a chance to participate, and you will encourage more thoughtful responses.

Students like to get off the topic. Sometimes that's fine. Sometimes it's not. Don't be afraid to get off the subject once in a while, especially if there is an opportunity for students to learn something important that isn't in the lesson plan.

Understand that what works with one group of kids may not work with another group. Be flexible.

Do not give up. When one thing doesn't work, try another.

Let students go to the bathroom, but never more than one at a time.

**You will have bad days. That's normal.
You will have great days. That's normal, too.**

Share yourself with your students. It will show them that it is okay to communicate and express emotions. If you are excited about becoming an aunt for the first time, tell them. If your grandmother is very ill, share your concern. Don't be aloof. **Be a real person.**

Expect the unexpected.

You have to have students' attention before you can teach them. Work hard to keep them interested by keeping your class period as varied as possible. Mix it up—some listening time, some doing time, some writing time, some reading time. It's hard to keep their attention if you're always doing the same thing in class.

Ask others for the materials and equipment you need. Scrounge for unneeded items from other teachers. Go to yard sales, the Salvation Army, and Goodwill. Ask people you know. It's amazing what you can get from people when you tell them you're a teacher!

Dealing with student attitudes toward testing can be a challenge. Some students will be apathetic, while others will be so anxious that they can't function properly. There are no magic answers for how to handle the problem. Experiment. Do your best.

Don't criticize children for being immature. They are *supposed* to be immature. They are children.

If "Read the chapter and answer the questions at the end" shows up in your lesson plans several times a week, you need to make some changes. The students probably aren't learning much.

When students complain about teachers, yourself included, remind them that part of education is getting along with and learning from many types of people.

If you think more experienced teachers never felt overwhelmed enough to cry, or feel like crying, you are wrong.

Don't do something in the classroom unless you can see a reason for it. It may be fun to have fingernail painting contests or to watch funny movies, but what's the point? (There may be one. Just be sure you know what it is.) If you can think of no valid reason for an activity, don't do it.

Always have a box of tissues on your desk, even if you have to buy it yourself.

Don't fret too much if you don't get through everything in the curriculum. Very few teachers do.

> **Don't teach your students to be pessimistic about the future. Let them learn that somewhere else. Make them feel in your class that they can change the world.**

Have a backup plan.

Let students have input.

Give them choices—always worded so that, no matter what they choose, they are choosing something you would want them to do anyway. (You don't have to let them know that!)

Ask yourself, every day, "What's really important here?" Is it more important to eliminate gum chewing, or to teach kids to subtract? Is it more important to get students to use the correct heading on a paper, or to teach them to write clear, effective prose? **Try to stay focused on what is really important.**

Never, ever leave your classroom unattended. **Always get another teacher, counselor, or principal to cover your class.** It only takes a moment for something bad to happen.

If you really want students to hear you, ask for "their eyeballs." If they are looking at you, they are much more likely to really hear you.

> **Don't let grades become too important** in your classroom. Remember that a good grade won't guarantee a happy marriage or a successful career. **A bad grade doesn't mean a life of crime** or a career saying, "Would you like fries with that, sir?"

Whenever you can, do an assignment yourself before you give it to your class. You will discover any problems with the lesson, and you will be able to help students more effectively with any difficulties they encounter.

Don't slam your hand on the overhead projector when you're angry. It's breakable.

Don't fall into the trap of doing the same things exactly the same way every year. **Re-experience your material**. Try reorganizing or approaching a topic from a new direction. That way you and what you are teaching will remain fresh, lively and spontaneous.

Never lecture all period. No one—no matter what age— likes to listen that long.

If you want their attention, whisper.

Don't succumb to the temptation to teach to the test. **Teach to the students.** Focus on teaching them what they need to know and giving them the skills they need.

If you are taking over for a teacher in the middle of the year, make the classroom yours. Rearrange the furniture. Bring in plants. Make new bulletin boards. Put your new "fingerprint" on the room to demonstrate a change.

Always have pens or pencils for students to buy or borrow. Yes, they should bring their own, but sometimes it just isn't worth making an issue of it.

> **Act out of the conviction that your teaching matters. Believe that you will make a difference. You will.**

Set high but attainable standards for your students, and stick to them. Students usually perform to the level of their teachers' expectations. They (and, surprisingly, parents too) will try to whittle your standards down, but if you continually model high expectations, most students will work to meet them.

Go to workshops. Take classes. Learn as much as you possibly can about both your subject matter and the art of teaching.

Be positive!

DEALING WITH DISCIPLINE

DEALING
WITH
DISCIPLINE

Many otherwise excellent teachers have failed in the classroom because they couldn't learn how to deal effectively with discipline. Discipline is a difficult part of teaching, and— like it or not—it is often what makes or breaks a teaching career. An out-of-control classroom is not a classroom where learning takes place, nor is it a healthy environment for students or the teacher.

But how does a person learn to have what is called "good discipline" in his or her classroom? A number of suggestions follow.

Listen to the old advice, "Don't smile until Christmas." It may be exaggerated, but the basic message is a good one. It's much easier to start out tough and loosen the reins later than it is to try and grab the reins after a class is running out of control. In other words, **it is much easier to lighten up than to tighten up.**

Be friendly toward your students, but don't try to be friends. Always remember that you are the adult.

Be fair.

Don't list 26 rules on the board and spend hours going over them. The students won't remember them. If a student has six classes, each with 26 rules, he or she has 156 rules to keep straight on any given day. That's just not realistic.

Decide what are the absolute basic, nonnegotiable principles or rules for your classroom—no more than three or four of them. Carve these in stone (or write them in permanent marker). Then stick to them absolutely.

Let students know that you are always willing to listen to complaints and suggestions, and that you will change a policy or a grade if the student presents a good argument. However, insist that students present their arguments in a mature, calm manner, either on paper or personally—and **NOT while you are trying to teach class.**

This guideline will help you separate students with serious complaints from chronic complainers or tantrum throwers. Students with legitimate concerns will talk to you after class. Students who just want to avoid responsibility for their actions usually won't bother. Neither will those who just enjoy entertaining the class by arguing with the teacher.

Find an experienced teacher in your department whom students like and respect. Turn to that teacher when you need advice about discipline.

Enforce consequences consistently, but don't be ridiculously rigid. It's okay to make exceptions in unusual situations. **You are in control.**

Use humor whenever possible, at least at first, in dealing with cell phones and other contraband in the classroom. One teacher says, "Please remember that all cell phones and other electronic devices need to be turned off and stored properly during the duration of the flight. Thank you." After that, her seventh graders love reminding each other that they can't have their electronics during the teacher's "flight," and it rarely is a problem.

Be sure you know your school's policy about electronics in the classroom. In most schools, students may have them, but they are not to be used in class. If students violate the rule, the teacher can confiscate the item for the student to pick up after school. Be very clear about the policy before you take any action.

Your job will be much easier if you win the respect of the "problem" students. Others will fall in line behind them. (However, be careful not to give them special treatment, or you will risk alienating the rest of the class.)

If you feel yourself starting to dislike a student, take action immediately. If you allow dislike to take over, you can be sure the student will sense your feelings. The results will not be positive.

To help stop your negative feelings, find a way to talk to the student as one human being to another, about something other than class. Ask about the band pictured on a student's T-shirt. Ask his opinion about a new TV show on Monday nights. Ask about all the commotion in the hall last period. When you approach the student kindly, in a personal way, you are much more likely to find something to genuinely like in the person.

Seek **cooperation** rather than **obedience.**

Begin class immediately. Take roll later. Otherwise you will lose the students right off the bat.

Develop a system that lets you access things quickly. **You don't have time during class to look for a file or staple a set of tests.** While you are looking or stapling, students will find ways to keep themselves busy—and it probably won't be by getting right to work on their homework assignment.

Trust your "gut." If something doesn't feel right, it probably isn't.

Never, ever get into arguments with students in front of the class. Tell angry or belligerent students that you will talk to them after class. If they persist in trying to start an argument, calmly repeat your request. Refuse to take the bait.

Some students thrive on getting the teacher upset, just to entertain the class. Don't give them that satisfaction.

Don't raise your voice if a group is getting too noisy. Instead, speak more softly.

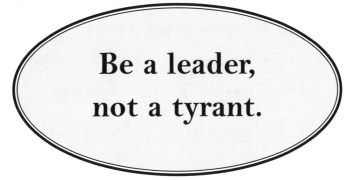

Never tolerate disrespect from the students. **Expect** respect and **show** respect.

> **If a child does wrong,**
> **fault the behavior,**
> **not the child.**

Always treat students politely and with respect. You may feel like swearing, smacking someone or ranting and raving. **Do not.**

Trust your students until you have reason not to—but keep your eyes open. Be trusting but not naive.

Detention can be an excellent opportunity. Many teachers have won over some of their worst problem students by assigning them detention—and then visiting with them informally, one on one. Getting to know students and showing an interest in them often works wonders in changing classroom attitudes.

Remember that *limits* help make a child feel safe.

Know when to play dumb. Sometimes it's better not to see a note being passed or not to hear a muttered comment.

Be aware that, even if you teach high school classes, your students are children. Even the oldest, the brawniest, the most mature, the most eloquent, the most confident is still a child. **Do not, then, be surprised at anything your students do.**

It is important to understand that, with some students, you are rewarding them when you reprimand them in front of the class. These students have learned that negative attention is better than no attention at all. Discipline students in private, one on one. Give them time to calm down before assigning consequences.

Tell your class that you, not the bell, will dismiss them. This may seem a small matter, but it will help you keep control of your class. It reminds students who is in charge.

Think of teens and preteens as caterpillars in cocoons, slowly breaking out of their shells, suddenly forced to deal with unfamiliar bodies and minds. Just as a newly released butterfly must adjust to its new body, which includes longer legs and huge wings, the developing teen must deal with big, clumsy hands and feet, changing body parts and unforgiving pimples. Try to remember what it was like to go through puberty. **Be kind.**

The most important teaching technique you can learn is **classroom management.** Without it, nothing else you do will matter. It's sad but true.

Learn to recognize that "something is going on here that we don't want the teacher to see" look.

Be careful what you notice. If you don't have time right now to deal with students smoking, don't walk into a restroom with smoke pouring out the doors.

Remember that if students see that you see something, you have to act. Once in awhile, it's better not to see it.

Be flexible, but not breakable.

Some teachers effectively use a **point system** to help in classroom management, taking points away for infractions and adding them for good behavior. Some use a point system for the class as a group, letting them earn a game day or other reward when a certain number of points are reached. If you decide to try a point system, be sure that it is simple and doesn't require too much maintenance time.

> # Students are not the enemy.
> # Never forget that.

> Don't rely on sending students to the office as a disciplinary technique. You will only become identified as "someone who can't handle his students." If you need help, try first to get advice from a teacher you respect.
>
> Send only your most extreme cases to the office. Rely on the office as a last resort—probably no more than three or four times a year, total.

If fights in the hallway scare you, don't be embarrassed. They scare a lot of people. Know your school's policy about what to do. Figure out a plan of action **before** you are faced with a fight.

When dealing with drugs, violence, or bullying, remain calm and call for assistance.

If a student comes to you with a problem that is confidential, honor that confidentiality—**unless the problem is life-threatening in any way.** (And sometimes students really do want you to intervene, despite what they say.) It is your job to try to keep them safe.

> **Never embarrass or humiliate students,**
> **especially in front of their peers.**

A key component in classroom management is the **individual relationships you establish with students.** Yes, greet them at the door with their names and a smile. Yes, ask them about their interest in baseball or the concert they attended. Yes, try to find out why someone is always so sleepy or seems depressed. If you can establish positive, caring relationships with most of your students, they are far more likely to behave and do their work and learn—not because you are a stern taskmaster but because they want to cooperate with you and don't want to disappoint you.

Don't get really mad at your class more than five or six times a year. **If an angry speech or stern lecture is extremely rare for you, the students will sit up and take notice.** If they hear one every day, they will learn to tune you out.

Don't threaten, unless you mean to follow through. If you threaten to keep the whole class after school, for example, the students won't believe you. You will just damage your credibility.

If you are having to deal firmly with an angry student, **never move toward the student.** Instead, state your desire calmly but firmly and then **turn away,** as though you expect the student to follow your instructions. That gives the student a chance to save face, and the confrontation is less likely to turn ugly.

> ## Do what you say you will do.
> If you are scrupulous about it,
> you will have far fewer problems
> than teachers who do not.

Modeling the right way to handle a situation is often more effective than school suspension or calling parents. Sometimes students really don't have the tools they need. Talk with a student about different ways to approach a situation, different words to use.

A technique that can also be effective is a "do over" or an "instant replay." If a student says something inappropriate or behaves inappropriately, simply have him "replay" the situation. Often the replay will give him the attention he craves, while also making it clear that you are the one in charge.

If your talks with a student about his or her behavior are getting you nowhere, **try getting a counselor** involved. Don't ignore the problem. A counselor's approach can be helpful, and it's worth trying before resorting to the principal's office.

Stop fights immediately.
Get help from other teachers or security people if you need to.
Your job is to keep kids safe.

Keep your sense of humor. Always.

Understand that bullying is an art form. Students who bully have mastered hiding it from parents, teachers, and administrators. If you discover it, it has been going on for awhile. Get involved immediately.

Pay attention when a student's behavior or attendance patterns change. Something may be seriously wrong. Something may be going on at home—an illness or a divorce, for example. Try talking to the student and/or referring the student to a counselor.

The student might also be the victim of bullying or cyber bullying. Be aware that students who suddenly want to help you during lunch or after school may be trying to avoid other students—another possible sign of bullying. Know your school policies, and get help. Remember that bullying is harassment and has legal ramifications.

If you hear students talking about bullying or cyber-bullying, become actively involved in stopping it.

Reward good behavior. It doesn't take much. Sometimes all it takes is just one jelly bean or a pat on the back.

Learn that you can agree to disagree. **Not all disagreements can be resolved.**

COMMUNICATING WITH PARENTS

COMMUNICATING
WITH
PARENTS

Communicating effectively with parents is often simply a matter of common sense. Tell them what is going on in your classroom—and why. Treat them the way you would like to be treated as a parent. The ideas that follow can be helpful guidelines.

Remember that **parents are not the enemy.** Even the worst parents in the world usually want the best for their children, even if their actions may seem wrongheaded and counterproductive.

Remember that **students usually get home before their parents.** If you leave a concerned message or send home a note, the parents may never see it. If you don't hear from them, try calling them at work, or at night.

If parents are blowing up at you, be quiet and listen. They are not going to hear anything until they calm down, so let them vent. (Phrases like "I understand what you're saying" help, too.)

Communicate with parents often, both formally and informally. It's a good idea to begin the year with a note or e-mail to parents telling them that you are happy to have their child in your class and that you look forward to a great year. Invite them to e-mail or call if they ever have questions, concerns, or comments. Follow that up with weekly e-mail updates about what's happening in class. Try to get a positive note to parents before you need to enlist a parent's help.

> # When communicating with parents, try to start and end on a positive note.

Keep a folder on your computer just for **e-mail correspondence to and from parents.** Keep the messages for at least the entire school year. It is good documentation if you should ever need it.

When parents e-mail, **be prompt** about getting back to them, even if it's with a short, "I received your e-mail and will respond as soon as possible." Then make sure that you do respond within 24-48 hours.

Be careful how you say things in an e-mail message. E-mail does not show inflection. Reread your message before you press "send," especially if you are feeling angry or frustrated. You might even consider waiting until the next morning to send something you feel strongly about.

In any kind of message to parents, show concern, and show you are aware of the child's strengths. Stay away from words or phrases that indicate judgment. Just give the facts. An example: *I just want you to know that Johnny did not do the book report that was assigned on September 16 and was due today. I gave him the opportunity to come to lunch study hall to finish it and turn it in for a late grade, but he chose not to attend. I spoke with him about how this will impact his grade. I feel concerned that Johnny's grade does not reflect what a good reader he really is. If you have any questions or concerns, please contact me. Thank you for your support.*

Don't take parental attacks personally.

Okay, *try* not to take parental attacks personally.

When meeting with parents at their request, allow them to speak first so that you can fully understand what their concerns are.

If you develop a positive relationship with parents, students are the ones who will benefit most. However, you will also benefit by having allies in the difficult job of helping young people succeed.

Ask parents to let you know if something significant occurs in their child's life that might impact his behavior at school. Knowing what's going on helps you give a child a little extra TLC when needed, or, at the very least, do no harm. (You don't want to come down hard on a child for not paying attention in class the day after her pet rabbit dies.) Parents like knowing that you care about their child's emotional well-being.

Create an information form to use for parent conferences. Fill it in before the conference, and go over a copy of it with the parents during the conference. This will help you organize your thoughts ahead of time, keep the conference focused, and leave you with a written record of what was discussed.

Remember that you and parents have the same goal: their child's well-being and success.

Only believe about half of what students say about home. Hope that parents do the same about school.

Involve parents as much as you can and keep them informed. When a student is not meeting the expectations in your classroom, academically and/or behaviorally, get in touch with the parents right away. Express your belief that you and the parent, working together, will help the child to be successful in the classroom. It is difficult for parents not to agree when you are talking about working together for their child's success.

Send home good news. Set aside time regularly to make positive calls to parents, or to write positive notes. (You can write a note in two minutes. One per day adds up to 180 per year.)

Tell how well a child is doing in your class, or that he got the highest grade on a test, or that you really appreciate the fact that she does her homework regularly—anything that can lead to a positive relationship with the parents. Many parents have never had someone call or write with good news about their child.

Let parents know that you check your school e-mail only once a day, and at what time. (Pick a time that works well for you.) Parents will then know when to expect a reply.

When students fail to show up to take make-up tests twice in a row, some teachers have the students sign the blank test and attach a note saying what they were doing instead of taking the test. If parents later complain about missing test grades, teachers can then show the child's signature and personal explanation for the zero.

If you are having trouble with a particularly difficult parent, a fringe group, a demanding organization, or anyone else connected with your school, start documenting all your conversations. Make a note of the date of the conversation, who was present, and what was said. In the event of complaints, legal action, negative publicity or other action, your notes could prove very useful.

Give parents as much information as possible so that they can be proactive and there are few surprises. If possible, make weekly grade reports available to parents through e-mail.

If a parent becomes confrontational in an e-mail, suggest that you discuss the issue with the parent in person. By setting up a meeting time, both you and the parent have time to think about the issue and possibly calm down a bit. It also gives you time to decide if an administrator or counselor should sit in on the meeting.

Proofread everything you send home. Right or wrong, you may lose a parent's respect if your messages are sloppy and incorrect.

FITTING IN

FITTING IN

There's more to being a teacher than just going to your room and teaching. You also have to be part of a department, a school and a school district.

Your job will be easier and more enjoyable if the people you work with are friends and allies. It is possible to learn something from nearly every adult in a school system. Take a look at the following tips for fitting into your school environment.

> ## Make a friend in your department or grade level.
> Glean ideas from her, raid her files, give her your undying loyalty and friendship—and maybe some lunches and milkshakes, too.

Never degrade other faculty or staff members in front of students. Call them by their proper names and speak respectfully of them, regardless of the situation.

Keep a stack of note cards handy. Make time to dash off thank-you notes to deserving colleagues, administrators and students. They will appreciate them.

Don't offer your opinions the first year, unless asked. Listen and ask questions. Learn how your school works before you jump in with suggestions for reforming the educational system.

Make friends with the school secretary. Secretaries have more power than you might suspect. Many of them practically run the school.

If you find yourself feeling alone or frustrated, check into an online community like the National Middle School Association's Middletalk. Some of the most dedicated, sharing, state-of-the-art people at all levels of education are willing to share on these sites. They can be a valuable resource.

Behave like a grown-up.

> **Don't extend faculty meetings with too many questions that reveal your rookie status. Ask a trusted veteran later.**

Learn how to operate and maintain all equipment—
computers, white boards, projectors, copy machines, etc. Don't depend on others to operate them for you.

Work hard.

You may be smart. You may have wonderful ideas. You may have plans for changing the world of education. Just remember that, no matter how much you think you know, you don't know it all. **Keep your ideals, but know that you will learn a lot in your first year or two of teaching.**

TAKING CARE OF YOURSELF

TAKING CARE
OF
YOURSELF

Teaching is a hard job. It is hard to be "on" day after day after day, especially if you have a cold or didn't sleep well or just feel generally out of sorts. It takes energy to motivate others and to deal with dozens of different personalities, learning styles, abilities, levels of accomplishment and family backgrounds.

You don't want to be a victim of teacher burnout before you have really begun. It is essential that you take steps to preserve your energy and enthusiasm for teaching. Try some or all of the ideas that follow.

Never make major writing assignments due the day before vacation. **You need a vacation, too.**

Most new teachers are sick a lot their first year. Don't imagine that you are dying if you are, too. You just need to build up immunity.

You will spend a lot of time in your classroom. Make a comfortable spot for yourself. If you need a high stool to perch on as you talk to a group, get one. If a comfortable pillow in your chair will help, buy one. Invest in colored paper clips or bright file folders or a *Far Side* desk calendar—whatever will make your area feel comfortable and pleasant to you.

Don't expect much of a social life until summer. You probably won't have time for one.

Don't feel guilty cutting into the front of the cafeteria line. The students don't have to go back to the classroom, eat, grade 30 tests before next period, check the mail in the office, call a parent, pick up an overhead projector from the library, and fill out six forms for the principal—all in 25 minutes. You aren't a student anymore. **You deserve certain privileges,** just as you now have certain responsibilities.

Don't sweat the small stuff.

Invest in a simple tool box. It's sometimes easier and faster to fix a loose screw yourself than to wait for a custodian.

Take time out for yourself. Set aside time regularly for something you enjoy—taking a dance class, knitting, playing on a soccer team, for example. A teacher **with** a life is better than a teacher **without** a life.

Don't try to be an interior decorator. Let students do the bulletin boards, unless it's something you really enjoy. You'll have more energy for other things.

Keep a journal. It will help you vent, let you brag to yourself about your accomplishments, and become a place for you to record memorable incidents. (Really, *do* this. Someday, you may wind up with a book of your own!)

Don't watch too many Hollywood movies about teacher success stories. They will only make you feel inadequate. Remember that the movies are only loosely based on real life. They don't show you all the ordinary days.

Sometimes it's okay to say "No." In your enthusiasm, do not take on too much. A tired or stressed-out teacher is not the most effective teacher. Know your limits.

Keep learning. Go to conferences, take classes, read. To be a great teacher, you must remain an avid learner.

Wash your hands often, with soap and water.
You will catch far fewer colds.

Take home only work you plan to actually do. Never take papers you think you *might* have time for. You won't.

If you don't have a chance to go to the bathroom until fourth period every day, you might want to **think twice about that third cup of coffee** in the morning.

> **Feel glad that you are doing one of the most important jobs in the world. Your impact may not be felt for a while, but trust that you are having an impact on the future, through the young people you teach.**

Keep an emergency folder with **generic lesson plans** for substitute teachers. If you come down with the flu, the last thing you want to do is drag yourself out of bed to write out detailed lesson plans.

Make a "good stuff" file for yourself. There will be days when you wonder, "Why didn't I become a stockbroker? I have absolutely no talent for teaching." On those days, dig out the file with the good stuff in it: the note that says, "You're my favorite teacher," or the evaluation from the principal that says, "Excellent lesson!" or the note that just says, "Thanks."

Exercise, eat right, and get enough sleep at night. **Being fit is half the battle.**

Keep **latex gloves** handy for medical emergencies in class or on the playground.

A sense of humor is more valuable than the best lesson plan.

Designate at least one day of the weekend as a "No Schoolwork Day."

A Few Words of Wisdom

A FEW WORDS
OF WISDOM

Teachers who have been around awhile have learned a few things about teaching over the years. It usually pays to listen to their advice.

There's an amazing amount of important "stuff" that is never mentioned in college classes. Some of this stuff can make or break a teacher's career. Learning to listen and learn from your colleagues is a wise idea.

Consider the following words of wisdom from experienced teachers.

Find something to like in every student. Know that there *is* something in every single one.

Don't be afraid to share yourself with your students. However, there's a difference between telling endless stories of your years as a high school football star and telling the students one story about an experience you had playing football.

If you teach in a small town, be aware that your behavior is probably public knowledge. If you snap at a waitress, people will know. If you get caught speeding, people will know. If you hang out at the bars a lot, people will know. Like it or not, your actions in your private life will affect your credibility and effectiveness in your professional life.

Ask for help when you need it. However, don't ask other people to do your job.

> Think things through carefully before you buy a house in the neighborhood where you teach. You may not want to explain all your life choices to one of your fifth graders who lives across the street.

Don't try to make your students like you. The irony is, if you don't really care, they WILL like you.

Don't be drawn into (and definitely do not solicit) student gossip, especially concerning a fellow teacher or administrator. When students complain about another teacher, don't take part in the criticism. Encourage them to discuss any problems with the teacher herself.

Avoid situations that involve being alone with a student outside the classroom—for example, taking him or her home from school or working late together on sets for the school play. When you talk to a student one-on-one at school, be sure the door is open and that others are always nearby. You will be less likely to leave yourself open to criticism or unwarranted charges.

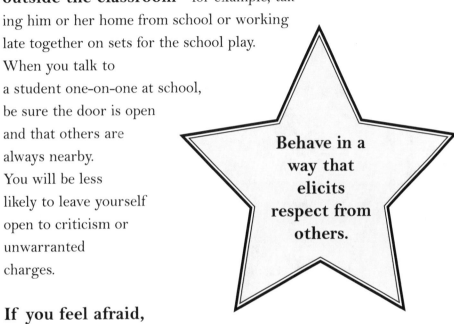

Behave in a way that elicits respect from others.

If you feel afraid, pretend you are brave.

If you feel crabby, pretend you are cheerful. If you feel unequal to a task, pretend that you can do anything. Often, pretending to feel a certain way will help you to actually feel that way.

> Look at yourself through the eyes of others.
> You can be fashionable without being risqué.
> Your friends may not raise an eyebrow to see
> your thong underwear sticking out of your
> low-rise jeans. A student or a parent may,
> however, get a different message.

If you are close in age to your students, be especially careful not to become too familiar or casual with them. Never flirt with them. **Maintain some distance and dignity.**

Don't complain to your students about how poorly teachers are paid or about how awful your job is. The classroom is not the place for it.

Know that whenever you pull into the school parking lot, whatever may be going on in your personal life, **you are in the role of teacher, mentor, and role model.**

Avoid discussing students with other teachers if there is any chance at all of being overheard. (Note: **There is almost always a chance of being overheard.**) Be discreet.

Don't assume that being liked is the same as being respected. Respect will take you much further in the classroom.

Remember that you don't have to **like** all of your students in order to **care** about them.

Ask for the materials and equipment you need from the administration. All they can do is say, "No." Have all the information available like where to order, the cost, and your justification for the expense.

> **Remember: Technology is a great tool,**
> **but it is not always appropriate.**
> **Chalk still works.**

Dress professionally. It will help students, parents and other teachers see you as a professional. It may even help you see yourself as a professional. (If you are very young, it will also help distinguish you from the students.)

Think outside the box.

Understand that students may remember little of what you teach, but much of what you model.

More books for teachers from Cottonwood Press...

Read author Gary Rubinstein's hilarious account of his disastrous first year of teaching, and then see his gradual but steady transformation from incompetent rookie to award-winning teacher. An honest and humorous look at the real world of teaching.

ISBN# 978-1-877673-36-8

With gentle humor, author Suzanne Capek Tingley gives practical suggestions and sound advice for working with parents more effectively.

ISBN# 978-1-877673-72-6

www.cottonwoodpress.com